Emperor Justinian
Byzantine Empire circa 555

Empress Theodora
Byzantine Empire circa 550

King Louis XVI

Queen Marie Antoinette

France circa 1778

Emperor Napoleon & Empress Josephine

France 1804

Prince Albert

England circa 1860

Queen Victoria

England circa 1870

Queen Elizabeth
England 2012

Prince Philip
England 2012